TABLE OF CONTENTS

ABOUT THE AUTHOR

Robert is a certified Raja yoga instructor, meditation teacher and a plant based chef. Robert is committed to helping others achieve their hearts greatest desires. Through his own healing journey he discovered the true path to wellness and vitality. His work involves taking the wisdom from the ancient rishis in yoga and combining it in with our modern lifestyle. These nature based protocols are designed to bring more energy into daily life. You can find inspirational yoga videos, travel vlog's, healthy recipes and more on his YouTube channel **theinfinitecup**

PREFACE

This book has been a long time coming. A lesson on procrastination. A journey of self-discovery. I have worked endlessly to compile all of the best knowledge of the real yogic practices into one book. I believe I have done my best to also persuade you into making yoga a part of your daily life. If yoga is already a part of your daily life I encourage you to take your meditation practice deeper. The beauty of this tradition is that there is no limit. We are discovering our infinite potential. This book is intended to be a manual of the soul. With this knowledge anyone can discover their own unique abilities. We are here to change the world.

One breathe at a time.

Chapter 1

WHAT IS YOGA REALLY?

Taking a vivid look at this modern world, it is apparent that things have changed drastically. Most people are accustomed to thinking that they can only find fulfillment and happiness outside of themselves. If I'm not mistaken, about 87% of the world's population think this way, and it's becoming increasingly alarming. More importantly, it's doing more harm than good to us. We are now living in a world that limits our belief in such a way that we are now unfortunately wired to believe that only outer attainments can give us what we want.

It is difficult for us to visualize a state of complete calmness and repose in which thoughts and feelings cease to swim in perpetual motion. We do not know that, it is through such quietness that we reach a level of joy and understanding that our outside forces can't possibly give. There is no doubt that ordinarily, our awareness and energies are directed outward to the things of the world, which we think bottles up our fulfillment, however we must learn to tap deeper and more subtle levels of awareness if we would solve the puzzle life throws at us.

"Yoga is a simple process of reversing the ordinary outward flow of energy and consciousness so that the mind becomes a dynamic center of direct perception, no longer dependent upon the fallible senses but capable of actually experiencing truth."

Okay now let's look at it in a more ordinary sense. Yoga is an art as well as science, because it offers practical methods for controlling body and mind, thereby making deep meditation possible. Unless it is practiced intuitively and sensitively, it will yield only superficial results. Here, you can see that Yoga surpasses the system of bodily postures-Hatha Yoga, which most of us in the West confuses it to be. Yoga is primarily a spiritual discipline.

Don't get me wrong. I'm not in any way trying to antagonize Hatha Yoga. The body is part of our human nature, and must be kept in shape, so it doesn't hinder our spiritual obligations. The higher teachings of Yoga take you beyond techniques, and show you how to direct your energy in such a way as not only to harmonize you with divine consciousness, but to merge your consciousness in the infinite. As we proceed, I'll shed more light on it. The word Yoga itself means "Union," of the individual spirit with the Universal spirit. Though many people confuse

Yoga as being only physical exercises, which is actually only the most superficial aspect of Yoga, there are various paths of Yoga that leads towards the goal of unfolding the infinite potentials of the human mind soul. Each one of these paths is a specialized branch of one comprehensive system.

Let's quickly check them out together; there are only six:

1. **HATHA YOGA:**

Hatha Yoga is basically a system of physical postures. Its purpose is to purify the body, giving you awareness and control over your body's internal states and preparing it fit for meditation. Hatha Yoga practice emphasizes proper diet, processes to internally purify the body, proper breathing and regulation particularly during the Yoga practice, and the exercise routine consisting of bodily postures.

2. **KARMA YOGA:**

Karma Yoga is quite spiritual. It is a selfless service to others as part of one's larger self, without attachment to the results; and the performance of all actions with the consciousness of God as the doer. According to James Lochtefeld, Karma Yoga is the spiritual practice of, "selfless action performed for the benefits of others." It is a path to reach a profound spiritual liberation through your work. It is a rightful action without being attached to fruits or being manipulated by what the outcome might be. It is basically a dedication to your duty and trying your best to be neutral to outcomes, either positive or negative.

3. **MANTRA YOGA:**

Mantra Yoga is to do with centering your consciousness within you through the repetition of certain universal root words representing sounds in a particular aspect of spirit. Mantra yoga uses mantras to awaken you and deepen the meditative aspects of a physical yoga practice. It engages your mind through focusing on sound, duration and number of repetitions. The main purpose of the repetition is to get closer to the divinity within you, and create positive vibrations that benefit you and everyone who is listening to your chants.

4. **BHAKTI YOGA:**

The path of the heart. Surrendering with devotion through which you strive to see the love and divinity in every living being thus maintaining unceasing worship. It is ultimately the practice of devotion. Using sacred transcendental mantras to soothe the soul and cleanse our heart purifying our entire being.

5. JNANA (GYANA) YOGA:

This basically is the path of wisdom, which emphasizes the application of discriminative intelligence to achieve spiritual liberation. Jnana is actually considered the most difficult Yoga paths because of its requirements for great strength of will and intellect. Success is achieved in this path by steadfastly practicing the mental techniques of self-questioning, reflection and conscious illumination that are defined by Four Pillars of Knowledge.

6. RAJA YOGA:

Raja translates to Royal. This path encompasses all of the other yoga traditions into one. This path is the pursuit towards independence, self-confidence and assurance. Likewise, a Raja Yogi is autonomous, independent and fearlessness. Raja Yoga is the highest path of Yoga, immortalized by Bhagavan Krishna. At the heart of the Raja Yoga system, balancing and unifying these various approaches, is the practice of definite, scientific methods of meditation which enable you to perceive from the very beginning of your efforts, glimpses of the ultimate goal. The basic premise of Raja Yoga is that your perception of the divine Self is obscured by the disturbances of the mind.

Chapter 2

ABOUT YOGA AND MEDITATION

My intentions are only to illuminate you on "Yoga" routine or teach you some new amazing steps that you probably would not find on the internet or any "Yoga" class. My plan was to get to your mind and get to know you even more. How can I possibly do that when the closest I am to you is this lovely piece of literature you are reading right now? Trust me, this is more spiritual than physical, and I'm not talking about Voodoo here. It's just what it is. What's the closest thing to you right now? Nope, it's not this book. It's not even your shirt. It is that very oxygen you are breathing in. It is so close that your eyes can't even catch a glimpse of it. Believe me when I tell you, I am closer than that very oxygen you are breathing in.

So what's the point? I just taught you something any other piece of literature will probably never teach you; the history is as important as the thing itself. So, how about you start applying that to everything you do. Who knows, you just might become even smarter than you think. Research says it's a confidence booster as well, so you just might want to add it to your To-Do list.

So what brought about the word "Yoga"?

According to history, *Yoga* has been in existence for over 10,000 years. It has been speculated to have originated from India. The word *Yoga* is said to have been first mentioned in the oldest sacred texts, the Rig Veda. The Vedas were collection of texts containing songs, mantras, and rituals to be used by Brahmans, the Vedic priests. Shortly afterwards, the Yoga culture was subtly redefined and developed by the Brahmans and Rishis (mystic seers) who made a documentation of their practices and beliefs in the Upanishads, an enormous work containing over 200 scriptures.

Amongst the over 200 scriptures, the most renowned is the Bhagavad-Gita, which was composed around 500 B.C.E. The Upanishads took the idea of ritual sacrifice from the Vedas and internalized it, teaching the sacrifice of the ego through self-knowledge, action (karma yoga) and wisdom (jnana yoga). During the Classical period, Patanjali defined the first systematic presentation of *Yoga* known as the Yoga Sutras. It was written sometime in the second century. This written piece organized the practice of *Yoga* into an eight-limbed path containing the steps and stages towards obtaining Samadhi, or enlightenment.

So, just in case anyone asks you who the father of Yoga is, you can simply tell the person

Patanjali is often considered the father of Yoga and his Yoga-Sutras still profoundly influence most styles of modern Yoga.

During the Post-Classical period, just after Patanjali, —Yoga masters introduced a new system of practices, designed to rejuvenate the body and prolong life. They rendered the teachings of the ancient Vedas obsolete and embraced the physical body as the means to achieve enlightenment. This brought about the development of Tantra Yoga, with radical techniques to cleanse the body and mind to break the chains binding us to our physical existence. This newly developed practice led to the rise of what we primarily think of Yoga in the West-Hatha Yoga.

During the Modern period, in the late 1800s and early 1900s, Yoga masters started migrating to the West, trying to attract attention and gain followers. This began at the 1893 Parliament of Religions in Chicago, when Swami Vivekananda compelled the attendees with his lectures on Yoga and the universality of world's religions. The adaptation of Yoga to the West still continued slowly, until Indra Devi opened her own studio in Hollywood in 1947. Owing to this, many more western and Indian teachers have become pioneers, projecting Hatha Yoga and gaining millions of followers. Hatha Yoga now has many different schools and styles, all nailing the many different aspects of Yoga.

Okay, I should probably take a rain check on this here, because the last thing I want to do is bore you with too much history. But face the fact— don't you feel smarter with all the information you just read? I believe now you can eloquently educate anyone about the history of Yoga. I think I just added to your knowledge. Well, what more can I say, you are welcome. But I'd rather you thank me later, when I am finally done exposing you to the amazing world of yoga!

Let us not miss out on the important things, especially for you. I know you are very serious about making Yoga a part of your live rather than following the trend of seeing it as just a physical exercise. So we have to touch every aspect, which the eight limbs provide the pathway.

Chapter 3

THINGS YOU PROBABLY DON'T KNOW ABOUT YOGA

THE EIGHT LIMBS OF YOGA

Firstly, let me say that the eight limbs of yoga form a moral or ethical code to help you live happier, and of course, liberated life. This is the core of what yoga is all about.

They are: Yama, Niyama, Asana, Pranayama, Prathyahara, Dharana, Dhyana and Samadhi.

❖ YAMA

Yama basically focuses on how you relate with others. This first limb refers to practices that are primarily concerned with the world around you and the way you interact with your world. Yama is expressed as five moral constraints:

1. Ahimsa (non-hurting)

2. Satya (truthfulness)

3. Asteya (non-stealing)

4. Bramacharya (moderation)

5. Aparigraha (generosity)

You can see that these five moral constraints are all about the way you relate with others; the gestures you project to others. It's nothing personal.

❖ NIYAMAS

Niyama focuses on self-relationship, and can also be considered with your actions towards the outside world. Niyama is traditionally practiced by those who wish to travel further along the

Yogic path, which I strongly believe you are one of those people. Niyama is expressed as five observances:

1. Sauca (purity)
2. Santosa (contentment)
3. Tapas (self-discipline)
4. Svadhyaya (self-study)

5. Isvara Pranidhana (surrender to the divine)

Clearly, you can see that these five observances focus mainly on self-dispensations, which could also affect your action towards the outside world.

❖ ASANAS

Asanas are basically postures practiced in Yoga. These postures help you develop discipline and concentration. The idea behind Asana is, to be able to sit in comfort, so you are not inconvenienced with aches and body pains. It specifically means the sitting position you would take for the practice of meditation in a rather relaxed manner.

❖ PRANAYAMA

The word Prana in its ordinary sense means energy, which ultimately, is the very essence that keeps you alive. Prana also describes breath, as in breathing. Pranayama are breathing techniques that are aimed at controlling the vital force, helping you feel alert and calm. The different breathing techniques routine alters the mind in a myriad of ways, because it changes your state of being.

❖ PRATYAHARA

Pratya means to draw back or withdraw, and Ahara means insert or take in. So it basically refers to anything you take in by yourself, such as various smell, sights, sounds etc. Pratyahara focuses on the withdrawal of senses; a conscious effort to draw awareness away from what is going on around you. The internal focus allows you to see your internal processes such as cravings and emotions.

Pratyahara doesn't necessarily mean you have to lose the ability to hear and smell, or receive impulses from the external factors around you, it only changes your state of mind, so that you become absorbed in what you are doing, that things outside what you are focused on no longer appeal to you, at least for that very minute. It frees you from distraction and helps you focus singularly on what you are doing.

❖ DHARANA

Basically, Dharana means concentration; the ability to be able to concentrate after removing yourself from outside distractions. This is the stage you get to when you think you are meditating, but you aren't yet.

❖ DHYANA

Dhyana is the uninterrupted stage. It is the stage of one-pointed attention, where you become completely absorbed in the focus of your meditation, and this is the point where you are really meditating. A t this stage, you won't even have the thought that you are meditating because you'd be completely lost in your visual realization that the fact that you are meditating would not even cross your consciousness.

❖ SAMADHI

Most people know the word Samadhi as meaning bliss. It is a stage of profound interconnectedness with all living things. It is a stage where you have completely processed everything to the smallest decimal and you have found peace within your inner mind. It is a stage of realization- and it is because reaching Samadhi is not about escapism, floating away or being abundantly joyful; it is about realizing the very life that lies in front of you.

It is through the constant practice of these eight limbs of hatha yoga that you can realize your true existence, the realization that you are not separate from your surroundings, or that you are connected by a universal consciousness. With the exception of the last three limbs-Dharana, Dhyana, Samadhi, you do not need to practice these limbs in any particular order. Each one of them helps cultivate the development of the others.

I specifically decided to take you through this chronological route, so as to give you a lucid understanding of what I'm trying to achieve through this. There is a lot I'm yet to unleash because I believe in due process. In case I haven't told you already, my passion is to see you enjoy the journey not the end goal. I personally have read a lot of books that commented on some certain topics that I was interested in, yet only few of them compelled me to the very end. A lot of them got boring at some point and everything became so vague that I totally forgot what I had been reading from the start. Let this information sit with you, literally. Meditate upon it and see what resonates with you the most.

"We are all on this journey together just walking each other home" -Ram Dass

Chapter 4

THE EYE OPENER

I know you have seen a lot on television, social media and blogs that makes Yoga look pretty simple; more of roll out a mat, breathe, and stretch yeah? That is the way it looks on the surface.

I'm really not trying to scare you off. Avert the confusion please. I am not trying to confuse you after all I have romanced you with. Relax, we are still on the same page here. I'm just trying to open your eyes to some facts, that's why I titled this "The Eye Opener."

There is way more to Yoga than just making some fancy shape with your body. I just want to open your eyes to some things you need to take in before actually starting your Yoga routine.

"So you mean I still haven't known enough after all the history, learning about the limbs and everything you have written about?"

No, you still haven't and I want you to know, not missing the tiniest detail. Relax and trust me. These things will actually make your practice stick into a life-long routine. So let's get to it.

❖ Whoever told you it's about flexibility actually lied to you:

I know you see a lot on your Facebook timeline and Instagram feeds, that promotes Yoga being all about flexibility, or maybe you even have a friend who told you Yoga is all about flexibility. Everything is false, in fact, flexibility can actually cause some serious injuries that could affect your performance.

Perhaps that's why Sage Rountree says, "Not only might some of the more outwardly glamorous poses be completely out of your reach for structural reasons-your skeleton might prevent them-your athletic pursuits are yielding sport-specific tightness in your body that help you perform well."

So, instead of focusing on being flexible, I'd implore you to focus on striking a healthy balance between flexibility and strength.

❖ Foundation is very pivotal:

Wait a minute, are you the over-ambitious type? I'm not trying to mock you. I just want to know really because I am one too. If you are, you have to calm down here a little. I am not saying being over-ambitious is bad. My point exactly is don't beat yourself too hard. I know you can't wait to be a professional. Perhaps you even have the dream of building your own Yoga studio. It is not impossible, really! There is nothing impossible as long as you are determined and focused, however since you are just starting out, you should focus on the fundamental Yoga postures first. Spend more hours in basics classes, it will give you a solid foundation on which to build your Yoga practice.

❖ **Your tenacity is 100% vital:**

It is very easy to give up after the first class. In fact, a lot of people actually give up after the first class and it's not because Yoga is boring or too stressful. It's just because they are in the wrong place. Apparently, all Yoga traditions look similar on the surface, but they are not all the same. Each type of Yoga has its own vibe. Often times, you don't get to like every single type of Yoga or even the teacher teaching it. That happens a lot and it is okay. There are so many options to explore, you just need to find the one that works for you. Don't you worry, I am going to educate you on the types of Yoga and which one is best for you shortly.

❖ **Getting the right mat:**

Of course, it is not foreign to you in any way that you are going to need a mat for Yoga. Let me just be blunt with this. Don't go for a mat that will get all slippery when you start sweating, especially if you're practicing in power vinyasa classes. Don't worry, you will get to know what I mean by vinyasa shortly. Finding the right mat is very important.

❖ **When it becomes overwhelming:**

This is somewhat inevitable, it happens to every starter. You'd be overwhelmed with confusion at the initial stage, owing to the fact that your body is still trying to adapt to the new culture. It's just a phase everyone goes through. You'll get past it sooner than you think.

Chapter 5

FISH, FIND YOUR WATER

The word fish is actually a metaphor, and I'm going to take my time to explain what I mean by "Fish, find your water". The various fish groups account for more than half of vertebrate species. There are almost 28,000 known extant species, of which almost 27,000 are bony fish, with 970 sharks, 180 hagfish and lampreys. Okay, that is enough. What exactly, am I driving at? What I'm trying to say is that some fishes are wired for salt water, while some are wired for fresh water. Hence, a fish wired for salt water cannot survive in fresh water, and a fish wired for fresh water cannot survive in salt water, it is that simple.

There are different types of Yoga and each has its guide and who it is best for. To make Yoga enjoyable for yourself, you need to find your water, which is best for you. Let's get started on that.

Don't let the array of options scare you off. Don't forget, be tenacious. You just have to find the one that resonates with you and stick with it. Just because you don't like one doesn't mean you won't like the other, just be patient and let's find which is best for you.

❖ HATHA:

If you remember, we have actually discussed this when we started out. It's nothing different actually. It's all about the basics. It is a gentler form of Yoga that requires you to hold each pose for a few breaths. Basically, it teaches physical postures.

RECOMMENDATION: This type of Yoga is highly recommended for beginners, because of its gentle pace and it helps lay a good foundation if you are just starting out.

❖ VINYASA:

I personally love this one because of its dance-like way. If you remember the part I was talking about getting the right mat, and not the type that would get all slippery when you start sweating? Vinyasa can make you get pretty sweaty because unlike Hatha, it is actually dynamic and it links movement and breath together. It's a fast paced routine, you won't have to linger long in each pose and the pace is quick. It is often accompanied with music, according to the teacher's choice. The music makes stepping the sequence interesting.

RECOMMENDATION: If you are just starting out, I wouldn't advise you to take this class, at least for a start, except if you are a voracious exerciser. Mostly endurance athletes are drawn to Vinyasa because of its dynamic movement.

❖ IYENGAR:

Iyengar is actually a bit more like further mathematics with its complexity. Props from yoga blocks and blanket to straps will be your companion, helping you to work within a range of motion that is safe and effective. It is not as fast as Vinyasa because each posture is held for a period of time. Iyengar actually has levels. It is advised that even if you have been practicing other types of Yoga, it is better to start with a level one class in order to familiarize yourself with the techniques.

RECOMMENDATION: Iyengar is good for people who like to geek out about anatomy, movement and form. Also, it is good for people who are detail-oriented. It is great for those with injuries as well but it is required you consult your doctor first.

❖ ASHTANGA:

Ashtanga is for those who love challenge. It is quite challenging yet it has an orderly approach. Ashtanga consists of six series of sequenced Yoga poses, you will flow and breathe through each pose to build internal heat. The poses are performed in the exact same other in each class. You need not worry much about the poses, there will be a teacher to school you on that.

RECOMMENDATION: Ashtanga is actually for the brutal perfectionists, people who can cope with the strict guidelines.

❖ BIKRAM:

Bikram is a vigorous practice, there is no better word for it. It consists of a specific series of 26 poses and two breathing exercises practiced in a room heated to approximately 105 degrees and 40% humidity, so be prepared to sweat like hell. Bikram is a 90 minute standard sequence everywhere, so anyone new to Bikram should take it easy and take a lot of water before starting.

RECOMMENDATION: If you are new to Yoga, you might actually like Bikram because of its predictable sequence.

❖ HOT YOGA:

Hot Yoga is similar to Bikram. It is also practiced in a heated room. But teachers aren't constrained by the 26 pose sequence.

RECOMMENDATION: Hot Yoga is for intense sweat lovers. If you love to get drenched after a workout, Hot Yoga is good for you.

❖ KUNDALINI:

Kundalini is physically and mentally challenging. It doesn't follow the traditional Yoga pattern, it involves performing repetitive physical exercises with intense breath work, while also chanting, singing and meditating. Those who want to escape their internal hindrances, release the untapped energy residing within them and reach a higher level of self-awareness, find this soothing.

RECOMMENDATION: If you want to get something spiritual coupled with workout, you can try Kundalini.

❖ YIN YOGA:

Yin Yoga is just the opposite of Ashtanga. It is good for calming and balancing the body and mind. Its poses are held for several minutes at a time. Yin Yoga helps target ones deeper connective tissues, in a meditative way. Props are being used so the body can release into the posture instead of actively flexing or engaging the muscles.

RECOMMENDATION: It is definitely not meant for you if you are super flexible and if you have a connective tissue disorder. It is meant for you if you need to stretch and unwind.

❖ RESTORATIVE:

Restorative is pretty much slow paced. It involves slow-moving practice with longer holds to give the body the chance to tap into the parasympathetic nervous system, so the body can experience deeper relaxation. Props including, blankets, bolsters and Yoga blocks are needed to fully support the body.

RECOMMENDATION: Restoration is good for everyone and specifically for you if you have difficulties slowing down, or have perhaps struggle with anxiety. It helps calm your nerves and it is also good for recovering athletes.

Now, have you found your water? You can see that everything is not for you. To enjoy Yoga, you just need to find the type that resonates with you and stick with it. That way, it becomes more of a lifestyle.

Chapter 6
MEDITATION

It is not enough to talk about Yoga and not talk about meditation. I have been shedding light on Yoga styles, it's about time I started shedding light on Meditation, don't you think? Mind you, it doesn't mean I am done with Yoga. I'm not even close to being done in any way. Like I said, I'm taking you on a chronological ride, just so you wouldn't miss out the tiniest detail. I still have a lot to tell you about Yoga, yet I'd rather we take a rain check on Yoga and talk about Meditation, since one can't possibly talk about one and not talk about the other. Yoga and meditation work hand in hand.

WHAT IS MEDITATION REALLY?

Just like the asana practice of Yoga aims to control the body, Meditation is a practice that helps you control or train your mind. It is an activity which you just sit and allow your mind to dissolve. Meditation involves generating a witness state observing the emotions for the purpose of analyzing that state, the state could be anger, sadness, etc.

Meditation may also involve repeating a mantra and closing the eyes as well. The mantra is chosen based on your individual preference. This practice has a calming effect and directs awareness inward until pure awareness is achieved. The amazing fact about meditation is that, the rest in meditation is more profound than the deepest sleep you can ever have because by engaging in the practice of meditation, your mind becomes free from agitation and you will experience calmness.

The term "Meditation" is quite broad, however I promise to make sure I touch on everything that needs to be addressed so you won't miss out on anything. I presume you already know more than enough benefits of meditation, hopefully. Okay let me just highlight a few, just in case you don't know what I'm talking about.

BENEFITS OF MEDITATION

Meditation helps calm your mind.
Meditation gives you clarity on a thought.
Meditation aids your communication.
Meditation helps you discover your inclinations,
such as skills, talents, etc.
Meditation gives you the ability to connect to an
inner source of energy.
Meditation helps you concentrate effectively.
Meditation improves your health.
Meditation helps you fight against depression.

Chapter 7
MEDITATION FAQ'S

I must say that personally, I cannot think of an act more important in one's life than meditation. Meditation is the key to unlocking life's fullest potential and it has been my savior for years now. Before I started meditation, I had series of questions on my mind that took a while before I could get answer to. So I have compiled some of the questions and provided the answers for you.

IS MEDITATION REALLY THAT IMPORTANT?

First, it begins a process of multi-dimensional actualization which has a profound impact on your life. Impacts including balance, wakefulness, wholeness, and the ultimate fulfillment of being human.

HOW LONG SHOULD MEDITATION LAST?

Everyone has a peak level of tolerance. It is imperative that you pay close attention to this. Generally, meditation can actually last for as long as you want it to last, basically, it all depends on how long you can go. That being said, you need to know that it also possible to meditate too much. Even one hour a day may be too much for beginners. For a start, it is best to meditate for 15 to 30 minutes a day and while doing this, you must pay attention to your peak level of tolerance. If you are exceeding your peak, you might have to stop, re-access and stick with what works for you.

HOW OFTEN SHOULD I MEDITATE?

Meditation is actually a life-long practice. You should meditate on a daily basis. If you can meditate more than once daily, do. Being persistent in your practice generates momentum and makes your experience more natural and effortless. Mind you, you still need to pay attention to your peak level of tolerance. Don't push yourself too hard, follow due process. Determine the proper amount of meditation that you can practice daily to insure balance and wakefulness.

HOW LONG WILL IT TAKE TO START EXPERIENCING THE BENEFITS?

Often times, some of the benefits of meditation begins to unfold effective immediately. Benefits such as reduction in stress, which you will notice simply by closing your eyes and focusing within. When you wrap up your meditation and resume your daily life activities, you will notice a more positive experience. The more you practice meditation, the more the innate happiness and joy will be naturally experienced.

DO I NEED TO EMULATE THE MONKS TO PRACTICE MEDITATION EFFECTIVELY?

This question actually scared me off meditation for a while because I thought I needed to live as a monk in order to experience peace and bliss. The answer is No, you do not need to be a monk to effectively practice meditation. Spiritual teacher,

Master Charles Cannon, developed High-Tech meditation to make it easy for people in the modern world to practice meditation effectively while living active lives, in the comfort of their homes. So, you can be you and still practice meditation effectively.

CAN MY CHILD ALSO MEDITATE?

Yes! he or she can. Meditation has no age limit, it is suitable for everyone. For children, meditation is especially helpful to foster normal brain development, which will be of a great benefit as the child matures. Meditation has a profound impact on the brain and the developmental processes of the body.

WHAT IF I FALL ASLEEP WHILE MEDITATING?

It is very common to doze off during meditation and some believe that the brief sleep you get is actually restorative. It is not the goal, but if it is a byproduct of your meditation, that is okay. The more you practice meditation, you will experience new levels of consciousness. These levels are associated with increasing holistic

power and you may experience what is termed
Absence, which many confuse with sleep.
Consciousness is simply managing your process
until you have integrated the new level of power
and find yourself more wakeful again.

DO I NECESSARILY HAVE TO GET A TEACHER?

Meditation is actually not something you can
possibly bluff your way through. Just like you
need a teacher to teach you differential calculus,
it is also important you get a teacher to guide you
on meditation. The reason many people bail out
of meditation is because of how confusing it can
be for starters. Getting a teacher will help you
understand your experience, helps you see when
you are stuck and how to address it, points you to
the right direction and most importantly,
motivates you.

WHAT POSITION IS BEST FOR MEDITATION?

Actually, it is about trying out different positions
and figure out which one works for you. In this
case, you also need to find your water, you need
to find that position that helps you meditate
effectively. But for best results, I recommend you

sit back straight and without back support. You may sit on a chair or cross-legged on a cushion.

CAN I LIE DOWN AND MEDITATE?

This is not recommended for starters. Like I stated earlier, it is best to meditate without back support. Although, lying down while meditating for long periods can be very effective for advanced meditators. For an advanced meditator, if you are meditating for longer periods of time, it can be beneficial to begin in a sitting position for at least an hour and then have a period of integration while lying down. Actually, the main problem of lying down from the beginning is that you can easily fall asleep.

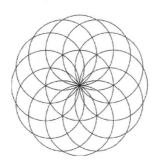

Chapter 8

TYPES AND TECHNIQUES OF MEDITATION

Just like I have been saying from the start, meditation is a practice that involves you focusing your attention inwards, often to relax and help you overcome anxiety.

As much as some people use meditation to relax, others pursue the practice as a lifestyle because they believe meditation is way deeper than just helping one relax and concentrate, they see it as a way of life. So they attack meditation as a means of following a particular religion.

Meditation is also somewhat complex because it has different types and techniques. Wait a minute, did I just say different types? I meant a lot of types and techniques, well, still different all the same. Since my aim is to be as coherent as I can possibly be so you wouldn't drift at any point, I am not going to bore you with too much information. I will be as brief and detailed as I can be. So, be still and keep believing in me. Let me drive you even further.

Some people actually find it pretty easy to utilize several types of meditation, but I will be blunt with you; meditation is just like yoga, you need to find your water as well. Mastering and practicing the one type that you find most beneficial will yield more significant brain adaptations. Singularly mastering the one that you find more comforting and sticking with it will do you so much good.

In addition, deciding which one is best for you is not something you do arbitrarily. You have to do some experimentation. You may want to try out a particular type a few times, and if you don't really like it, don't stop right there, move on to another type. The only way to find the type that best works for you is by testing the waters with some different techniques and observing how beneficial each one is.

"But, how do I find the right water for me when I don't even know the waters to try out and the techniques to use?"

Right, I totally get you. You just want to get started already and get it over with. Lets do it. Calm your nerves and believe in the process. Let's take this one breath at a time. I know you can find a lot of short and undetailed articles about meditation on the internet, but there is no rushing this. To attain excellence, one can't rush. You have to be still and enjoy the ride. So now let's slide to what we are really talking about.

THE TYPES

Remember the part where I said that meditation has several types? Yes, it really does but I really do not want to confuse you with the types at all. We both have come a long way to have you confused at this point. I'm still sticking with my promise of being as brief and detailed as I can be. So I'm going to make it a lot more easier for you by bringing everything together and fine-tuning everything in a rather coherent way.

The most popular types of meditation include:

❖ Mindfulness Meditation:

Mindfulness meditation started from the Buddhist teachings and is the most popular type meditation in the West. Mindfulness meditation focuses on you paying attention to your thoughts as they dance through your mind. You simply observe and take note of the pattern in

which your thoughts dance in your mind. It helps you combine concentration with awareness, by paying attention to your thoughts and being aware of what your thoughts are.

This type of meditation is actually good for you if you do not have a teacher to guide you because it is what you can easily and individually practice alone.

❖ Focused meditation:

Focused meditation involves concentrating using any of the five senses; eyes, nose, ear, tongue, and skin. For instance, you can focus on something within your inner self like your breath, or you can bring in external influences to help focus your attention.

It appears quite simple on paper but can be quite challenging, for beginners especially because it's will be quite difficult to hold your focus for longer than a few minutes if you are just starting out. The mind often wanders away, so to practice this type of meditation effectively, it is important to come drive yourself back to focus when you go off course.

It is highly recommended for you if you require a deeper level of focus in your life.

❖ Movement Meditation:

Are you thinking this means yoga because of the name? Well, owing to the fact that yoga ultimately deals with movement, you should but it's not yoga. Movement meditation practice is action based, it may include walking through the woods, feeding animals, gardening and other gentle forms of motion. It is a type of meditation that the movement guides your mind through.

Look within yourself. If you find peace in action and prefer to let your mind wander, movement meditation is good for you.

❖ Mantra Meditation:

Mantra meditation is well known in many teachings, including Hindu, and Buddhist traditions. Mantra meditation is a type of meditation that uses a repetitive sound to clear the mind. It can be a word, phrase, or sound.

Mind you, you don't necessarily speak out your mantra loudly or quietly. Is it still vague? Okay, this is the way it really works, after chanting the mantra for some time, you will be more alert and in tune with your environment. This allows you to experience deeper levels of awareness.

Most people enjoy mantra meditation because they find it easier to focus on a word, phrase, or sound. This type of meditation is good for you if you do not like silence and enjoy repetition.

❖ Transcendental Meditation:

Transcendental meditation is classified as —effortless‖ because it requires no mental effort or concentration and it is undoubtedly the most popular type of meditation around the world and it is the most scientifically studied. This type of meditation involves emptiness, introversion and calmness.

This practice is more customizable than mantra meditation, using a mantra or series of words that are specific to each practitioner.

This type of meditation is good for you if you like structure and want to take meditation as a lifestyle rather than a temporal practice.

❖ Spiritual Meditation:

Spiritual meditation is used in religions, such as Hinduism, Daoism, and Christianity. This practice reflects on silence around you and seek a deeper connection with your God; it is similar to prayer. It is basically, being still before your God.

This is ultimately based on your belief system. It is good for you if you want to attain a certain level of spiritual tenacity. It pushes you even deeper.

Chapter 9

SIMPLE MEDITATION TECHNIQUES

Developing a practice can be quite challenging at the initial stage because you'd get this feeling that you are too busy, you are unable to sit still, or you can't even hold your mind long enough. This feeling is very normal, nothing is wrong with you, but I have to tell you this, since you have determined to make meditation a lifestyle rather than just a temporal practice, you need to be intentional about it. Your body will definitely negate it, but you have to be strong-willed and get it over with.

I remember when I first started meditating, after the first few tries, I was challenging until someone told me that if I try practicing meditation for at least 10 minutes in a day, my life would change. At first I didn't believe it at all because I am always full of doubts as a person. But later I decided to give the theory the benefit of the doubt, so I tried it out.

So here are some life-changing benefits I derived from meditating for just 10 minutes daily as a beginner.

I BECAME THE MASTER OF MY THOUGHTS:

I had always been a slave to my thoughts until I decided to take meditation seriously and practice daily for 10 minutes. My thoughts had a way of enslaving me and stealing my joy. When I subjected myself to meditation, I began to become the master of my thoughts, I was no longer a slave to my thoughts like I initially was.

There were nights I would not be able to sleep as a result of being a slave to my thoughts. But ever since I started my daily 10 minutes meditation technique, the muscle of my mind was strengthened and it helped me quell my obsessive thoughts.

I BECAME MORE MINDFUL:

I remember how I reacted back then if things

didn't work out the way I had planned. I'd freak out pretty bad as if my existence depended on it. During my meditation, I learnt how to create space between my thoughts. It'd allow me to pause and find that space again before freak out irrationally.

IT HELPED ME BECOME FEARLESS:

Often times, you confuse fearlessness with being without fear, but that's totally wrong. Fearlessness means being brave. Observing this techniques taught me how accept life the way it is, so I can then make it what I want it to be. It takes being brave to do that. I became fearless to deal with what was not working in my life and trust me, it's what got me here.

I BEGAN TO MANIFEST MY DREAMS:

I came to the realization that, in order to manifest and create my ideal reality, I needed to know who I am and what I truly want in life. I actually struggled with finding myself for years and at times it led me into some serious depression. Meditation helped me get the clarity I wanted and it in turn helped me define the paths and steps I needed to take to get to where I am going. It is still of a tremendous help to me and I will forever be grateful for it.

Okay, I can actually go on and on about the benefits however I'd rather stop here since I still have a lot to teach you. Now let's go into the basic techniques. They are very simple and are not complicated in anyway. Trust me, you probably know some of these techniques already.

THE TECHNIQUES

Don't forget every good meditation practice must begin with finding your water, where you actually belong. This does not mean there is a wrong way to meditation. Trust me, there is no wrong way, it's just about you discovering what works best for you.

Ideally, your back is straight and your spine is aligned. But it is not necessary to sit on the floor or even to cross your legs. If you are unable to sit for any length of time, find a proper lying down position that would prevent you from falling asleep.

Here are some simple techniques to try out:

❖ **CANDLE STARINGTECHNIQUE:**

This is a powerful technique that helps you focus. If you have problem focusing while meditating, you can light a candle and stare at it. It helps you hold your attention for as long as you set your focus on the candle light. If your mind races while staring, don't you worry child, just observe what it is doing and let those thoughts release.

❖ **VISUALIZATION TECHNIQUE:**

Visualization technique is another easy and highly effective way of meditating. All you need to do is to picture an image or create a soothing setting in your mind and feed your focus on the picture. Let yourself embellish it as much or as little as you need to.

❖ MOMENT TECHNIQUE:

Moment technique is quite deep. Let me just teach you how to navigate through this technique. Close your eyes and begin to focus on your breath. Take a few moments here then allow your focus to broaden to your body and the sensations that it is feeling. Now expand your focus to anything touching your body, noticing those sensations. Lastly, expand your awareness to everything you can possibly hear and sense. Now reverse this process and come back, one step at a time to your breath.

❖ MANTRA TECHNIQUE:

I need not talk this over again, you already know what mantra is. But just for a reminder, it is all about repeating words over and over so you can find calmness and focus. The choice of word is entirely of your own coinage, you can decide to make up your own words, just make sure you feel good about your choice.

❖ THE OBSERVER TECHNIQUE:

This technique helps you become the observer of your mind. You can simply close your eyes and focus on the spot about an inch above of your eyebrows, known as —The Third Chakra.‖ Begin to watch what your mind and body are feeling, thinking, and doing.

In addition to these few techniques I have highlighted, you can also implore the use of guided meditation materials. There are hundreds of resources online that have a huge supply of guided meditations and music to help sooth your soul. You can check out my website theinfinitecup.com or Google Play, iTunes or SoundCloud for adequate guided materials.

This specific type of meditation practice has been of a tremendous impact on my spiritual, mental, physical, and emotional wellbeing, I have seen my emotional and mental state improve, calm, and expand. Begin with just 10 minutes daily, and you will see positive drastic changes in your life. Trust me, this is not me trying to sugarcoat anything or make you believe anything. Like I said earlier, I also had problems believing until summoned the courage to at least try it out. And now meditation has single handily changed my life for the better. Within just a few weeks you will begin to experience the benefits.

THE REAL DEAL

Now, this is the real deal. This is where I reveal all I have been holding back since we started. This is where I open your eyes to what Yoga and Meditation truly is and how you should exactly practice for maximum results.

Before we slide completely into the world of Yoga and Meditation, I'm aware that I haven't fully yet satisfied your curiosity as regards on Yoga itself, and that's what I am going to do right now.

Chapter 10

SATISFYING YOUR CURIOSITY

CAN YOGA INCREASE MY LIFESPAN?

Yes actually, Yoga can increase your lifespan if practiced as lifestyle. The effect of Yoga is one that can't be possibly analyzed totally, but to name a few, let's run through some:

Yoga prevents your cartilage and joint breakdown: It is a known fact that yoga takes joint through their full range of motion, which helps joint cartilage receive fresh nutrients, prevents wear and tear, and protects underlying bones. It also helps prevent degenerative arthritis and migrates disability.

Yoga increases your bone density and health: Apparently, many yoga postures require weight bearing, which strengthens and helps you ward off osteoporosis. Specifically, yoga strengthens arm bones that are vulnerable to osteoporotic fractures. And in addition, many research as shown that yoga practice increases your overall bone density.

Yoga helps clean your lymph and immune system: Practicing yoga aids the draining of your nymph, allowing your system to better fight infection, destroy diseased cell, and rid toxic waste in the body.

Yoga aids your blood flow: You are surprised right? Well, yoga does gets your blood flowing. It helps the circulation of your blood and the movements you make during the practice of yoga brings more oxygen to your cells. Twisting your body brings fresh oxygenated blood to organs, and inversions reverse blood flow from the lower body to the brain and heart. Yoga also increases your hemoglobin levels in red blood cells, which helps you prevent blood clots, heart attacks, and strokes.

Yoga helps regulate your heart rate: Classes such as power yoga can help boost your heart rate into the aerobic range. Research has shown that, yoga can lower resting heart rate, increase endurance level, and improve maximum uptake of oxygen during exercise. Those who practice breathe control are especially able to do more exercise with less oxygen. So regularly moving your heart rate into the aerobic range lowers your risk of heart attack and it can also relieve depression.

Yoga regulates your adrenal gland: The practice of yoga helps you lower your cortisol levels. If high, they compromise the immune system and may lead to permanent changes in your brain.

The cause of major depression, osteoporosis, high blood pressure, and insulin resistance these days has been linked with excessive cortisol. So yoga helps you lower your cortisol levels.

Yoga lowers your blood sugar: In people with diabetes, yoga has been found to lower blood sugar by lowering cortisol and adrenaline levels, encouraging weight loss, and improving sensitivity to the effects of insulin. Lowering blood sugar levels decreases your risk of diabetic complications such as heart attack, kidney failure, and blindness. Yoga improves your balance: Your regular practice of yoga increases your ability to feel what your body is doing and where it is in space and improves balance. Better balance could mean fewer falls. For the aged folks, this translates into more independence and delayed admission to a nursing home or never entering one at all.

Yoga calms your nervous system and helps you sleep deeper: The craziness of our modern society can tax your nervous system. Yoga and meditation encourages your turning inward of your senses and removal of stimuli, providing much needed downtime for the nervous system and better sleep.

Yoga gives your lungs room to breathe: It is a known fact that yogis tend to take fewer breathe of greater volume, which is both calming and more efficient. Yogic breathing has been shown to help people with lung problems due to congestive failure and improves measures of lung function, including maximum volume of breathe and efficiency of exhalation. Yoga promotes breathing through the nose, which filters, warms, and

humidifies air. This helps prevent you from asthma attacks while also removing pollen, dirt, and other things you'd rather not take into your lungs.

Like I said earlier, —just to name a few. Yoga has a lot of positive implications on your health and it can increase your life span tremendously. So making yoga a lifestyle is not just going to benefit your health wise but also increase your chances of living longer than you ordinarily would. There are still a lot of benefits to mention but I have a lot run through, so can only name the few I have named. But I believe with the little I have named you can see how beneficial yoga is. So, gorgeous why not make yoga a lifestyle and enjoy life even more.

DOES YOGA HAVE AN AGE LIMIT?

I really have lost count of how many times this question has popped up. The answer still remains the same and will always be, yoga has no age limit, no size limit, no height limit, no race limit, no complexion limit, and what have you? Yoga is for everybody.

I think this question is rather psychological. Apparently a lot of people find it difficult to do some certain things when they attain a certain age. They feel they are too old to play sport, go ice-skating, and all

If you feel you are too old and really nervous about practicing the general yoga class, many studios offer specific classes for different groups of people. There are classes for men only, single women only, older women people, and children. So it's basically all about finding your water. I'm sure there are classes around your neighborhood that offer yoga classes in respect to your age bracket. You just need to find one and get started. So stop thinking yoga is not for you, stop thinking you have outgrown yoga. Yoga is for everybody. You should get down with it.

DOES YOGA HAVE ANY SIDE EFFECTS?

Actually, this question is what scares people away from yoga. I know you have read a lot of mis information on yoga and they have perhaps answered this question wrongly; that is why you are still curious as to if yoga truly has side effects.

The research study conducted by Holger Cramer, Gustav Dobos, Department of Internal,

Integrative Medicine, Kliniken Essen-Mite, Faculty of Medicine, University of Duisburg-Essen,

Essen, Germany, and Carol Krucoff, Duke University, Durham, North Carolina, United States of

America was published in the scientific journal on October 16, 2013.

The authors said while yoga is gaining popularity in North America and Europe, its safety has been questioned in the lay press. The aim of this systematic review was to assess published case reports and case series on adverse events associated with yoga.

Medicine/Pubmed, Scopus, CAMBase, IndMed and the Cases Database were screened through February 2013, and 35 case reports and 2 case series reporting a total of 76 cases were included. Ten cases had medical preconditions, mainly glaucoma and osteopenia. Pranayama, hatha yoga,

and Bikram yoga were the most common yoga practices, headstand, shoulder stand, lotus position, and forceful breathing were the most common breathing techniques cited. In the study, 27 adverse events (35.5%) affected he musculoskeletal system, 14(18.4%) the nervous system, and 9(11.8%) the eyes. Fifteen cases (19.7%) reached full recovery, nine cases

(11.3%) partial recovery and in one case (1.3%) there was no recovery.

About 14 million Americans reported that yoga was recommended to them by a physician or other therapists.

So what do I have to say about this? Actually I do not mean to scare you in any way. I definitely did not bring you this far to tell you that if you do yoga, you are probably going to regret it for the rest of your life, definitely not. All I'm saying is, there are side effects but you have it under control if you follow the steps I instructed. Ultimately, find your water and stick with it.

According to the researchers, yoga should not be practiced as competition and yoga teachers and practitioners should never push themselves or their students to their limits. Beginners should avoid advanced postures such as headstand or lotus position and advanced breathing techniques such as kapalabathi. Practices like voluntary vomiting should perhaps be avoided completely as well.

As yoga has been shown to be beneficial for a variety of conditions, it can also be recommended to patients with physical or mental ailments, as long as it is appropriately adapted to their needs and abilities and performed under the guidance of an experienced and medically trained yoga teacher. Especially, patients with glaucoma should avoid inversions and patients with compromised bone and other musculoskeletal disorders should avoid forceful or competitive yoga forms. And also, yoga should not be practiced while under the influence of psychoactive drugs.

DO I HAVE TO CONTINUE MY YOGA ROUTINE FOR THE REST OF MY LIFE?

The decision to continue practicing yoga for the rest of your life is entirely of your own coinage. If you noticed it changed your life a way you never thought it would and you are happy about it, I need not to tell you to consider doing it for the rest of your life to ensure a prolonged benefit. On the other hand, if it has not remotely been of help to you, perhaps you should stop when you can't take it anymore.

Truthfully, yoga is worth making a lifestyle. Perhaps you should read the "FISH FIND YOUR WATER" part again. The amazing thing about yoga is that, if you can figure out the one that works for you, you'd want to do it for the rest of your life because it will become so enjoyable.

WHAT SHOULD YOU WEAR TO YOGA CLASS?

This is a question I love answering so much, because it is a very pivotal question; being ignorant about it can hinder your yoga practice. It imperative that you know the right thing to wear to class because picking the right yoga outfit improves your performance. I'm going to illuminate you on what to wear and what you should not wear.

Let's get to it…

Firstly, comfort and fit are key so you wouldn't be distracted while doing your poses by futzing outfit. I'm going to start up with what not to wear and why not wear them, and subsequently what to wear.

WHAT NOT TO WEAR

NO LOOSE SHORTS PLEASE: You can wear them while doing your sweaty runs at home but not for yoga please. I am pretty sure you want to feel extremely confident and free while striking your yoga poses and not being distracted by the feeling that someone might be seeing your private part. Short wears or loose shorts tend to bunch up when you make a swift move to a certain direction. You sure don't want to be distracted by having to pull your shorts down in order to cover yourself.

WHAT TO WEAR INSTEAD

I'd rather you go for fitted cropped or full length leggings. This will cover your body parts without having to worry about anything, and moreover, the material hugging your skin will absorb sweat and make it easy for you to strike your poses.

WHAT NOT TO WEAR

NO COTTON OR LACY UNDERWEAR: It is not that this fabric is bad, it just gets heavy when wet and you know it doesn't dry up easily.

WHAT TO WEAR INSTEAD

I'm sure you don't want to stay wet down there for an entire class session. I'd rather you go for some moisture-wicking briefs, or better still, go undies free.

WHAT NOT TO WEAR

NO OLD, THIN, HOLEY, OR LIGHT-COLORED PANTS PLEASE: I know you cherish that

comfy old pair of leggings you've had since heavens knows when. Don't you think it's played out already? That pant has seen better days already, so it's time to let it go. Also, check your pant for holes in the crotch or thinning material. You should as well avoid light-colored pants because no matter how thick the fabric is, they are always see-through; you really do not want people staring at your booty.

WHAT TO WEAR INSTEAD

You can wear black, navy blue, chocolate, or another dark-colored pair of leggings made out of durable material.

WHAT NOT TO WEAR

NO T-SHIRTS, LOOSE TANKS, AND SHORT TOPS: You should know already that t-shirts will definitely end up falling over your head every time you come into Down Dog. Loose tanks can also distract you if you are not the type that likes showing your belly.

WHAT TO WEAR INSTEAD

I'd rather you go for long fitted tanks because they stay put and keep you cover in all twisting positions. And go for a shirt with the proper fit instead of a loose one. You might want to try it out in the dressing room before buying it, to ensure accuracy.

WHAT NOT TO WEAR

NO REVEALING AND LIGHT-COLOURED TOPS: This one is ultimately for the ladies. I'm pretty sure you do not want a situation where your boobs will fall out of your shirt, definitely not. I understand that top might seem fit while you are walking around, but it just doesn't fit when you start moving around in different poses. So, please save yourself the embarrassment. And also, white or light-colored tops are also risky, especially if you know you get pretty sweaty.

This tops can be pretty revealing when you start sweating, so it's a no for me.

WHAT YOU SHOULD WEAR INSTEAD

A sport top that supports your body type will do. Dark-colored tops are good and make sure they are not see-through.

CAN PREGNANT WOMEN PRACTICE YOGA ?

This question is also a very controversial question because a lot of women actually don't want anything to sabotage their chances of delivering safely, totally understandable. But the truth of this is:

Yoga can be very beneficial during pregnancy, as long as you take certain precautions.

Yoga helps you breathe and relax, which in turn can help you adjust to the physical demands of pregnancy, labor, birth, and motherhood. It calms both mind and body, providing the physical and emotional stress relief your body needs throughout pregnancy.

Taking a prenatal yoga class is also a great way to meet other moms-to-be and embark on this journey together.

Here are some recommended guidelines:

* If you are attending a regular yoga class (one not specifically geared to pregnant women), be sure to the instructor that you are pregnant, and which trimester you are in.

* Don't do any asanas (poses) on your back after the trimester – they can reduce blood flow to the uterus.

* Avoid poses that stretch the muscles too much, particularly the abdominals. You are more at risk for strains, pulls, and other injuries right now because the hormone, which allows the uterus to expand, also softens connective tissue.

* From the second trimester on, when your center of gravity really starts to shift, do any standing poses with your heel to the wall or use a chair for support. This is to avoid losing your balance and risking injury to yourself or your baby.

* Steer clear of Hot Yoga – working out in an overheated room. Overheating can endanger the health of your growing baby.

* When bending forward, hinge from the hips, leading with the breastbone and extending the spine from the crown of the head down to the tailbone. This allows more space for the ribs to move, which makes breathing easier.

* Keep the pelvis in a neutral position during poses by engaging the abdominals and slightly tucking the tailbone down and in. This helps relax the muscle of your buttocks and the hips flexors, which can help reduce or prevent sciatic pain down the back of the leg, a common side effect of pregnancy. It also helps prevent injury to the connective tissue that stabilizes your pelvis.

* If you are bending forward while seated, place a towel or yoga strap behind your feet and hold both ends. Bend from the hips and lift the chest, to avoid compressing your abdomen. If your belly is too big for this movement, try placing a rolled-up towel under your buttocks to elevate the body, and open the legs about hip- width apart, to give your belly more room to come forward.

* When practicing twisting poses, twist more from the shoulders and back than from the waist, to avoid putting any pressure on your abdomen.

Go only as far in the twist as feels comfortable – deep twists are not advisable in pregnancy.

* Listen carefully to your body. If you feel any discomfort, stop. You will probably need to modify each pose as your body changes.

A good instructor can help you customize your yoga to suit the stage of pregnancy you are in.

Here is a list of yoga poses you can practice during pregnancy and how to go about it:

Vakrasana (Twisted pose)

* Sit erect with feet stretched in front (parallel).

* Inhale and raise your arms at shoulder level, palms facing down.

Exhaling, twist your body from waist towards your right moving head and hands simultaneously to the same side. Swing arms back as much as possible. Do not bend your knees.

* Inhale and come back to original position maintaining your hands shoulder level and parallel to each other.

* Repeat on other side.

Benefit - Your spine, legs, hands, neck are exercised along with gentle massage to abdominal organs.

Utkatasana (Chair pose)

* Strengthens thigh and pelvic muscles

* Stand erect with feet 12 inches apart. Keep your feet parallel to each other.

* Inhale for 2 seconds and raise your heels and arms at shoulder level, palms facing down simultaneously.

* Exhale slowly; sit in squat pose, on your toes. If not comfortable standing on your toes, stand normally keeping feet flat on the ground.

* Keeping your hands in the same position, inhaling, get up slowly and stand on your toes.

* Exhale, hands down and heels down simultaneously.

Konasana (Angle pose)

* Flexibility of waist and fat remains under control in the waist region

* Stand erect with feet 24 inches apart. You can do this asana with the support of wall.

* Raise your right hand up keeping elbow straight. Give a nice upward stretch and while you inhale, bend sideward towards your left. Exhale and come back and put your hand down.

* Repeat the same with other side.

Paryankasana (Ham's pose with one leg)

* Strengthens abdominal, pelvic and thigh muscles

* Lie down on your back. Straighten your legs. Keep your knees together. * Now, fold your right leg in the knee at the side of your posterior. Breathe normally. Hold the position as long as you're comfortable and repeat the same on other side. Straighten your leg.

* Repeat with the left leg.

Hast Panangustasana (Extended hand to big toe pose)

* Strengthens pelvic and thigh muscles

* Lie down on your back. Straighten your legs. Keep your body in one line.

* Your hands in T-position, palms facing down.

* Slide right leg towards your right side. Don't try very hard. Hold toe with your right hand if possible.

* Sliding your leg come back to original position.

* Repeat the same on left side.

Bhadrasana (Butterfly pose)

* Strengthens inner thighs and pelvic region

* Sit on the mat with legs fully stretched.

* Keeping the legs in contact with the mat, form 'Namaste' with your feet. -Sit erect, without leaning forward. Place your hands on knees or thighs. Hold the posture till the time you feel comfortable.

* Straighten your legs and repeat again.

Parvatasana (Mountain pose)

* Improves body posture, relief in backache

* Sit on the mat in sukhasna, padmasana or ardhapadmasana.

* Sit straight and while you inhale, raise your arm and join your palms in 'Namaste' position. Keep your elbows straight. Hands are near to your ears. Hold the position for a few seconds and come back to normal position again.

* Repeat 2-3 times

Yastikasana (Stick pose)

* Corrects posture, body gets stretched, relieves body tension

* Lie down on your back. Straighten your legs. Keep your body in one line. Knees and feet are

together. Feet point upward. Hands rest on the sides.

* Inhale and raise your hands; rest them on the floor and stretch upward. Push your toes out simultaneously.

* Exhale, raise your hands and come back into normal position.

* Repeat 3-4 times with in between breaks.

YOGA POSES YOU SHOULD AVOID DURING PREGNANCY:

Of course you know that all yoga poses are not meant for you since you are already pregnant.

You can't keep practicing the same yoga poses you used when you were not pregnant.

Naukasana (Boat pose)

Chakrasana (Wheel pose)

Ardha Matsyendrasana & (Sitting Half Spinal Twist)

Bhujangasana (Cobra pose)

Viparita Salabasana (Superman pose) Halasana (Plow pose)

Ultimately, you should make sure you consult your doctor before practicing any form of yoga. And also make sure you inform your yoga instructor that you are pregnant, so as to reduce chances of complications.

CAN YOGA HELP ME LOSE WEIGHT?

Yoga is great to develop flexibility and strength, we all know that. The big question here is: will it make you lose weight?

You've probably been planning it in your head to start practicing yoga full time right? But all you need is to be sure your effort won't be a wasted one if you start; you want if yoga can actually help you lose some weight. I get you totally.

Don Peers, the yoga guru extraordinaire says "if you do the more sedate styles, like Iyengar or slow Hatha, you essentially won't be lifting your heart rate a great deal. If you do the more dynamic styles like Ashtanga or a power yoga class, your heart rate can be lifted to the level of a cardio workout – you will be burning calories. That's on a purely physiological aspect. If you talk about yoga on a deeper level, all forms of yoga stimulate the glands and organs, making them more efficient."

Peers maintains that if the body is running at optimum, you'll naturally eat less food. "Also, some yoga has an effect on the 'bandha', which is the core, and as a result your stomach and intestines work a lot more efficiently and the digestive mechanisms work better. The more yoga you do, the better your body will function, and the more weight your body will disperse."

Besides that, because it is a breath practice, Peers argues it makes your body use oxygen more effectively and, if you are breathing better, you will end up eating less. "There are a few new studies about the effects of breathing and people who don't breathe properly are more stressed," he says. Stress eater, anyone?

So are there specific yoga poses that will help you lose weight?

Inverted poses reverse the gravity effect on intestines – when you're upside down your intestines widen and in turn move food through the body more efficiently. Secondly, because it drains the blood out of the legs it stimulates the whole lymphatic system. When you come down after the inversion, it recalibrates the lymphatic system, which is really beneficial for weight loss.

He also attests that twisting yoga poses squeeze the intestines, kidneys and liver, therefore making them function better. Not to mention the muscle you'll build with all the other poses, which in turn will help the body burn energy even when you're at rest.

Peers cautions, however, if you are starting out in yoga, you need to move slowly because you're prone to injury if you go too hard, too fast. And if you're moving at a slower rate, you might not lose weight initially because of that. "Tell someone to jump straight into an Ashtanga class and they'll probably never come back! I think power yoga is good to start with, but always be careful and move with control," he advises.

Fitness expert Richard Chew, owner of the Elixr Health Clubs, says that the fastest way to lose weight is not yoga or running.

"Food is the main factor in weight loss – what you're eating and how much," says Chew. "Yoga is an activity that will burn calories but as with everything, it depends on how much you do and what intensity. There's no magic trick. The main problem is that we eat too much sugar. Anything that says fat-free is full of sugar and then you get the fat for free afterwards."

His philosophy is to enjoy the exercise, so it doesn't become a chore.

"Most people start out very enthusiastically but overdo it and then quit a short while later. It's better to underdo than overdo. I recommend exercising 8-10 times a month for 30-45 minutes at a time. That way you'll be consistent, over a long period, which will create new habits and that's what will make long-term changes."

Chew says the best weight loss exercise combines resistance training with cardio training. So the perfect workout then is yoga plus running. It shouldn't be an either/or question.

"You get out of yoga what you put into it," says Peers. "I would say you should do yoga three to four times a week. If you want to do more, you get the benefits of doing more, like everything in life."

Need I say more? I think I have given you enough information already. I'd rather you start yoga effective immediately to lose that weight.

DOES YOGA REALLY HELP WITH DEPRESSION, STRESS AND ANXIETY?

I remember when depression first afflicted me, it was as though my life was over. It made me feel as though I was a product of an astronomical random chance that amounts to nothing, yes it was that bad.

According to research, the most common psychological disorder in the Western world is depression; around ten times more people are diagnosed with depression now than 70 years ago. Emotionally crippling, it can require years of expensive and time-consuming therapy and often medication to control it.

While counselling and medication will always be the preferred method for some, in most cases mild depression and low-level anxiety are the price we pay for busy lives juggling work and family in an age of constant digital bombardment. But there is a low-cost, easy and enjoyable alternative

to pills that can benefit us all mentally — a natural anti-depressant remedy that studies have shown boosts a chemical in the brain that is essential for good mental health.

You already know what it is; it's yoga baby!

Back in 2013, a study by Massachusetts General Hospital found that the deep physiological state of rest induced by the three yoga elements of postures, breathing and meditation produced immediate, positive change in immune function, energy metabolism and insulin secretion. Insulin is known not only for regulating blood sugar, but also for triggering the production of serotonin — the feel-good neurotransmitter that can be stimulated artificially by some anti-depressants, such as Prozac.

Yoga's effectiveness on depression, stress, and anxiety comes from its proven ability to release tension and lower cortisol levels — people who are depressed tend to have elevated levels of the stress hormone cortisol. Therefore, by simply improving your posture through practicing yoga can help improve your mood.

Here is a list of few yoga poses that can help you with depression, stress, and anxiety:

(see back of book for detailed pictures of all asana postures)

STANDING FORWARD BEND

How to go about it: Stand with feet parallel and hip-width apart, toes pointing forward. Breathe in and stretch spine upwards with arms straight above head and palms facing in.

As you breathe out extend body and hips forward, bending from the hips. Bring your hands towards the floor. If your hands can't touch the floor, lightly touch your legs. The body should be as close as possible to the front of your thighs.

Benefits: Improves your upper body circulation and calms yet energizes your body.

SEATED TWIST

How to go about it: Lie flat on your back, allow feet to relax and roll out, arms a little out to the sides, palms up. If necessary, you can place a cushion under your knees to support your lower back.

Benefits: It is helps you relax.

EXTENDED PUPPY POSE

How to go about it: Begin on all fours. Walk your hands out far enough so that, while keeping your arms straight, you can drop your chest towards the floor, keeping your hips over your knees and arms shoulder width apart. Place your forehead on the floor and pull your hips back towards your heels. Hold this position for a minute.

Benefits: It lengthens the spine, releases tension in your upper body and calms your mind.

HAPPY BABY

How to go about it: Lie on your back and bring your knees into your belly. Grip the outsides of your feet with your hands, open your knees as wide as you can and propel them towards your armpits. Gently push your feet up into your hands to create a good stretch.

Benefits: This pose opens and stretches your hips, realigns the spine and relieves stress.

LEGS UP WALL POSE

How to go about it: Sit sideways as close as you can to a wall and swing your legs up the wall so that your body is lying on the floor at 90 degrees to your legs. Do this pose after a challenging work-out or if after travelling by plane.

Benefits: It helps you relax and helps you with insomnia.

CAN YOGA HELP ME IMPROVE MY PERSONALITY?

Well, we both know how contemporary living plays havoc and you could say it's a necessary evil. Office politics, exams, competitions, family commitments, looking slim and trim are all social norms that stress us to the maximum.

And that's what it is people are reaching the highest form of stress these days and simply letting it be is leading people to higher rates of depression, violence, divorces, and suicide. And to curb such stress people in their droves are making it a priority to practice yoga be it at the gym, in parks and when time is a constraint in the comfort of our homes. So should you jump on the bandwagon too? It could be the difference between you being unhappy or happy. And what better way yoga is a great natural solution to many problems.

So, to answer your question, yes, it does help improve your personality tremendously through the following ways:

Stress Relief

Yoga provides the nice opportunity for a well-deserved break away from our stress triggers. And just like the effect of medication, only after a few minutes the stresses that were build up throughout the day can be greatly reduced.

Inner Peace

Have you ever seen someone who practices yoga? If you had to describe them in one word it can likely be —clam‖ and they take it with them where ever they go including in stressful times. Yoga promotes calmness and build mental strength and a positive outlook on life where you will find nothing will seem to faze you almost at all.

Cool Factor

Yoga has a —cool tag attached to it. And it seems everyone is doing it so you wouldn't want to also feel left out. And don't forget the fashion, being seen adorning your yoga pants and carrying your mat are symbol of your social status. And it's very comfortable to wear at that.

Weight Management

Most known yoga styles that of Hatha yoga consists of slow movements and you may question if you will ever lose weight. But hey, anything is better than nothing. And since yoga promotes strength in return helps shape your body by improving muscle tone. Also, as you grow in experience you can push yourself to burn more calories with the vigorous types of yoga like Power Yoga or sweat it out with Hot Yoga.

Increase Strength, Flexibility, and Balance

When practiced on a frequent basis yoga will help improve your physical fitness and reduce the chances of injury, pain, and medical mishaps. And is a great choice no matter what level of fitness you are at, for beginners you can start slow and easy, or if you have some experience you can challenge yourself with Power yoga. Also, you can alter poses according to your ability.

Correct Body Posture

Through constant practice, your body will automatically align. And not only can it correct health issues such as neck and back pain when you hold yourself upright, you feel and look confident. And others will notice it too with just one look, a perception of your well-polished personality is formed.

Improve Focus and Concentration

Often times, you stress about things that might happen in the future. Yoga makes you live in the moment. Beginners to yoga will struggle with this concept. I often found my mind wandering off too. But with practice and concentrating on how I move my body, perform poses switch between poses and watch my breathing while doing it all, I was able to stay in the moment. And not to mention the movement encourage blood circulation and with that the flow of oxygen through the body. This skill is transferable to any situation you face in your day-to-day routine.

Sound Sleep

It is a better option than most other exercises of such since they tend to over stimulate your body with its vigorous movements. The slow movements of yoga help relax the mind and body and exhaust all its remaining energy from the day. It provides the perfect downtime that helps prepare your body into sleep mode. Sound sleep means you'd be more energized for the following day.

Wow, I can't believe we've come this far. Well this is just the beginning. Hope you haven't drifted? Come back, come back...Let's continue on our journey.

I KNOW YOU HAVE DOUBTS

THE PROOF:

If you are still out there doubting the effectiveness and wonders of yoga and meditation, well, I'd say keep doubting and question everything in life.

The Buddhist philosophy holds that the problems and worries of everyday life can be eased by paying greater attention to what is happening in the present.

Researchers found this mindset, along with some light stretching and careful breathing, lowered stress levels far more than typical stress management techniques. An eight-week course of mindfulness was found to lower levels of stress hormones which can lead to high blood pressure. People asked to give a demanding presentation in front of clipboard-wielding people in white lab coats found the experience far easier to cope with.

The study's lead author, Dr. Elizabeth Hoge of Massachusetts General Hospital, said: —This is not just a fad, it has been around for thousands of years in Buddhist countries, and we have found it helps people in a very practical sense. We think it works because it helps people create a little bit of distance between their thoughts and themselves, seeing that their worries will pass.‖

The research, published in the journal Psychiatry Research, included 89 patients with generalized anxiety disorder - a condition of chronic and excessive worrying. They were randomly divided, with half taking an eight-week mindfulness course.

In two-and-a-half-hour sessions, these people went through the three main tenets of mindfulness, first focusing closely on their breathing and then different parts of their body, before doing some gentle Hatha yoga stretching exercises. The meditation was followed by 'homework' such as eating a meal mindfully by focusing on every bite. When tested for levels of adrenocorticotropic hormone, triggered by stress, their levels were lower than the other half of the group.

These people had done a more traditional stress management course over the eight weeks, involving advice about how to use their time, nutrition and sleep, with recorded tapes to take home.

The researchers found the mindfulness group were also better able to cope with a stressful short-notice eight-minute public speaking task in front of a panel of people wearing white lab coats, taking notes and holding a large video camera, followed by a five-minute mental arithmetic test.

Dr. Hoge said: —we were testing the

patient's resilience, because that's really the ultimate question - can we make people handle stress better?'

Resilience is defined as the ability of individuals to adapt successfully to acute stress and adversity, maintaining a state of psychological wellbeing or returning to one rapidly.

The people who meditated also had lower levels of inflammatory reaction to stress in the body, which can lead to type 2 diabetes.

The findings avoided having a placebo effect, as both groups of people were given stress management courses and did not know which were of interest to the authors. They were also measured for stress before the interventions.

Mindfulness may have existed for centuries, but testing its effectiveness has previously proven difficult. One previous study showed that mindfulness meditation training may cut the risk of relapsing into depression.

However a study by Oxford University found the fashionable technique could affect memory, with people performing worse in tests after a 15-minute mindfulness session and even falsely imagining items within the test.

Dr. Hoge said: —Mindfulness meditation training is a relatively inexpensive and low-stigma treatment approach, and these findings strengthen the case that it can improve resilience to stress.

Now to Yoga:

I think I have said more than enough about the benefits of yoga, but for you who still have doubts, I will start with what Science says about yoga:

Current research suggests that a carefully adapted set of yoga poses may reduce low-back pain and improve function. Other studies also suggest that practicing yoga (as well as other forms of regular exercise) might improve quality of life; reduce stress; lower heart rate and blood pressure; help relieve anxiety, depression, and insomnia; and improve overall physical fitness, strength, and flexibility. But some research suggests yoga may not improve asthma, and studies looking at yoga and arthritis have had mixed results.

One NCCIH-funded study of 90 people with chronic low-back pain found that participants who practiced Iyengar yoga had significantly less disability, pain, and depression after 6 months.

In a 2011 study, also funded by NCCIH, researchers compared yoga with conventional stretching exercises or a self-care book in 228 adults with chronic low-back pain. The results showed that both yoga and stretching were more effective than a self-care book for improving function and reducing symptoms due to chronic low-back pain.

Conclusions from another 2011 study of 313 adults with chronic or recurring low-back pain suggested that 12 weekly yoga classes resulted in better function than usual medical care.

Still not enough? Yes I know. I know it's going to take more than this to convince you tha yoga really does work. Trust me I have prepared for this:

I am fully aware that it is natural to reach for scientific terms in an attempt to legitimize yoga's therapeutic benefits; thus we hear, for example, that backbends fight depression by stimulating the adrenals.

Science supports several possibilities for how yoga helps with depression. Studies have found that it reduces levels of cortisol (a stress hormone that's also secreted by the adrenals), which is often elevated in people with the disease.

And a study in India found that a yoga program that included asana, pranayama, and meditation raised levels of serotonin and lowered levels of monoamine oxidase; two neurochemicals involved in depression.

Yoga is known to induce the relaxation response; to lower the activity of the sympathetic nervous system's "fight or flight" mechanism and increase the work of the more restorative parasympathetic system; this characteristic does help with depression. This means yoga is a natural method to relive stress and maintain healthy blood pressure. This ancient practice has been around for over 10,000 years and is specifically designed to enrich ones mental, physical and spiritual wellbeing.

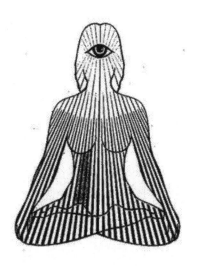

Chapter 11
YOGA POSES FOR YOU

Mountain Pose - Tadasana

Half-Moon Pose – Ardrha Chandrasana

Tree Pose – Trikonasana

Warrior One Pose – Virabhadrasana

Warrior Two Pose - Virabhadrasana

Forward Fold – Uttanasana

Standing Backward Bend – Anuvittasana

Firm Pose – Vajrasana

Table Pose -Prasthasana

Downward Dog – Mukha Svanasana

Side Leg Stretch – Padmasana

Front Leg Stretch – Uttanasana

Cat Stretch – Marjariasana

Forward Fold – Uttanasana

Cobra Pose - Bhujangasana

Bridge Pose – Sarvangasana

Shoulder Stand – Sarvangasana

Corpse Pose – Shavasana

Lotus Pose - Padmasana

Chapter 12

THE GUIDE

(YOU ARE NOT ALONE)

To be honest, I almost gave up on yoga when I first started as a result of excruciating pain. The pain was so severe that I had to bail out for a couple of weeks so I could heal. During my healing process, I had to read up on why yoga hurts when it's supposed to give positive feedback.

I guess you have possibly felt this way too right?

Well, according research, more than 20 million people are down-dogging across the West these days, pressing heels to mats in an attempt to reap yoga's supreme health benefits. Research has also found that if yoga is practiced incorrectly, it can cause you some pain.

WHAT YOU SHOULD KNOW

While most yoga injuries aren't severe and go unreported, more serious issues do occur, including strains and sprains, fractures, dislocations, and, in rare cases,

bone spurs, sciatic nerve damage, and stroke. But according to yoga experts, injuries can happen any time, in any sport, or even walking down the sidewalk, and scary injuries are rare. Most yoga injuries develop gradually over years of consistent over-stretching and misalignment. As with any physical activity, the safest approach to yoga is to learn how to practice the poses correctly and stay in tune with your body to avoid overdoing it.

To get the lowdown on the most common yoga injuries and some specific tips for addressing them, yoga instructors Steven Cheng of Yoga Union in New York, Julie Skaarup of Sol Yoga in Frederick, Maryland, and Jeni Livingston of Body Space Fitness in New York illuminated me on this topic and I'm going to do the same now:

WHERE IT OFTEN AFFECTS AND THE WAY OUT

Wrists: When it comes to the wrists, it's all about leverage. Placing all of the body's weight in the wrists when the hands are on the mat can lead to muscle and joint injuries.

It is advisable to distribute your body weight through both hands by spreading them wide and pressing through the fingers. In down dog, push the hips back to decrease the angle of the wrists to the floor. In arm balances, such as crow pose, look to see that the elbows are stacked directly over the wrists.

Elbows: Joint pain in the elbows can result from bending them out to the sides. While it may be easier to execute, lowering down with outward-pointing elbows can stress the joint and can also put undue stresses on the wrists.

It is advisable to bend your elbows in a pose (particularly plank), keep your elbows tucked alongside the ribs as you bend them, and make sure your elbows creases face forward. If this is difficult, begin with the knees on the floor.

Shoulders: When you raise your shoulders up toward the ears (like when moving into up dog), you should stop using the supporting muscles in the arms, shoulders, and neck. Shrugging compresses the shoulders, which can cause muscle injuries. Even worse: It's easy to injure the shoulder girdle or rotator cuff by over-extending.

You should be careful not to pull too hard on your shoulders in stretches, and always keep your shoulders held back and down away from your ears.

Ribs: Twists are awesome for releasing tension, but if done improperly they can overextend or bruise the intercostal muscles (the muscles in between the ribs).

Here, it is advisable to lengthen upwards through your spine before twisting. Imagine that someone has a string attached to the crown of your head and is very gently pulling you up toward the ceiling. Twist to the point of feeling a stretch but not past it, even if you're flexible.

Lower back: Lower back pain is the most frequently cited yoga injury, and teachers speculate that it's likely the result of rounding through the spine in poses like forward folds and down dog.

Rounding causes your spine to flex the opposite way that it's supposed to, which can cause disc problems in addition to that achy feeling post-class.

Before bending, imagine lengthening your spine up and away from the hips to avoid rounding. Still struggling to stay on the straight and narrow? Try bending your knees in poses like forward folds and down dog, since the culprit could be tight hamstrings. During seated forward folds, try sitting on a blanket or block to take pressure off your lower back.

Hamstrings: Many of us have tight hamstrings, so it's easy to pull or over-stretch them in poses like forward bends.

Down dog and lunges are great ways to stretch YOUR hamstrings (just remember to go slowly and work at your own pace). If you have any kind of hamstring injury, try laying off poses that extend through the back of your body and legs until the injury heals.

Hips: It is actually easy to over-extend your hips range of motion in splits, warrior poses, and wide-legged forward folds, which might tear the muscles of your inner groin or inner thighs.

A good rule of thumb is to make sure that your toes are pointed forward in any pose where your hips is squared off in the same direction. Imagine there are headlights attached to the front of your hips and that you're trying to keep the area straight ahead of you illuminated at all times.

Knee: Knee issues often plague even experienced yogis well after class. A common culprit of pain is the cross-legged position. Flexibility carries from your hips first; if your hips are tight in the pose, your knees will be the first place to feel pain or tension.

If you are regularly bothered by knee pain, avoid sitting in cross-legged position or full lotus for long periods unless your hips are already very flexible. Placing a block or rolled-up blanket under your knees in cross-legged positions can also help reduce strain. Any time your knee is bent in a standing pose (such as warriors I and II), look to see that there's a vertical line from your bent knee to the heel; this ensures that the body is bearing weight properly.

Neck: Head and shoulder stands can be the worst culprits for neck pain and injury. Repeatedly and incorrectly placing pressure on your neck in poses such as shoulder stand and headstand can compress your neck and put pressure on your cervical vertebrae, resulting in joint issues and, in some cases, loss of neck flexion.

It might be best to avoid full inversions all together. If you already practice the pose without props, make sure your shoulder blades are drawn down and back so they're safely supporting your body. Most importantly, never jerk your head once you're up in the pose, because it can destabilize your body, possibly causing a fall.

Chapter 13

MINDFUL LIVING

Mindful living or mindfulness as you know means maintaining a present-moment awareness of your thoughts, feelings, bodily sensations, and surrounding environments. It involves acceptance, meaning that you attend to your thoughts and feelings without judging.

The first is a mindful life is worth the effort. It is a life where you awaken from the dream state you are most often submerged in — the state of having your mind anywhere but the present moment, locked in thoughts about what you're going to do later, about something someone else said, about something you're stressing about or angry about. The state of mind where you're lost in your smartphone and social media.

It is worth the effort, because being awake means you're not missing life as you walk through it. Being awake means you're conscious of what's going on inside you, as it happens, and so can make more conscious choices rather than acting on your impulse all the time.

Being mindful is a process of forgetting, and then remembering. Repeatedly. Just as breathing is a process of exhaling, and then inhaling

repeatedly. Mindful living isn't just one thing. It's not just meditation. Nor is it just focusing on the sensations around you, right now in this moment. I've found mindful living to be a set of related tools, perhaps all different ways of getting at the same thing, but each useful in its own regard.

I know you are probably wondering why I am talking about mindful living or mindfulness. Well, it is essential I do because you cannot achieve this goal without being awakened from your dream state.
Take it or leave it, you have been sleeping for a very long time, and I need you to be fully awake. I need you to wake up and come out, come back to life and let us both achieve this ultimate goal. You are not alone on this, we are together.

The choices life gives you at times, makes you want to stress over everything and get bitten pretty bad, I understand all that. It can be pretty messy and tough at the same time to choose not to stress over something or even think about it. But you have to come to the realization that your happiness and well-being is ultimately your choice.

You can choose to be in control of your feelings. If you get a bad news, you can choose not to let it weigh you down. Wait a minute, this is not some motivational speech. It is just the fact. You need to be mindful of what you harbor in order to experience the full liberation you so long so much for.

Often times you get so lost in what is going on around you and you channel all your strength of focus on things that are mostly negative, like the person who got on your nerves, the bad report you got from work and all that. I need you to take that away right about now and let us do something productive with this.

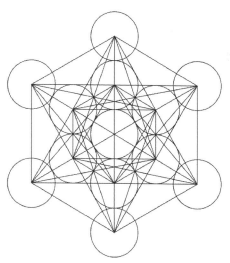

Chapter 14

The Core Principles of Yoga

Yoga is a meditative means of discovering dysfunctional perception and cognition, as well as overcoming it for release from suffering, inner peace and salvation.

Yoga is the raising and expansion of consciousness from oneself to being coextensive with everyone and everything.

Yoga is a path to omniscience and enlightened consciousness enabling one to comprehend the impermanent (illusive, delusive) and permanent (true, transcendent) reality.

Yoga is a technique for entering into other bodies, generating multiple bodies, and the attainment of other supernatural accomplishments.

I want you to enjoy this, and most importantly, I want to clear whatever doubts or negative information you probably have as regards "Yoga". I am aware that many people think "Yoga" is only a physical exercise where people twist, turn, stretch, and breathe, you are probably one of them, however these are just the most elementary aspect of this LIBERATING ROUTINE. "Yoga" imbibes a way of life with its emotional integration and spiritual elevation that breaks you free from all sort of chains you might find yourself in. We are the ones we have been waiting for. With the power of yoga we can achieve anything in this world.

Namaste

Robert Breton

ACKNOLEDGEMENTS

This is a HUGE thank you to everyone and everything that made this book possible.

A short list of people to give credit to:

My teacher: Bhavani Girard

My Momma: Dawn Miller

My Beloved : Alison Berry

The best photographer: Nick Noel

The countless souls who have inspired me.

Mother Earth

Bhagavan Krishna

AUM – SHANTI - AUM